Pebble® Plus

Dance, Dance, Dance

Tap Dancing

by Kathryn Clay

Consulting editor: Gail Saunders-Smith, PhD

Content consultant: Heidi L. Schimpf,
Director of Programs and Services
Joy of Motion Dance Center
Washington, D.C.

CAPSTONE PRESS
a capstone imprint

Pebble Plus is published by Capstone Press,
151 Good Counsel Drive, P.O. Box 669, Mankato, Minnesota 56002.
www.capstonepress.com

092009
005618CGS10

Library of Congress Cataloging-in-Publication Data
Clay, Kathryn.
    Tap dancing / by Kathryn Clay.
    p. cm. — (Pebble plus. Dance, dance, dance)
    Includes bibliographical references and index.
    Summary: "Simple text and photographs present tap dancing,
including simple steps" — Provided by publisher.
    ISBN 978-1-4296-4005-3 (library binding)
    1. Tap dancing. I. Title.
GV1794.C57 2010
792.7'8 — dc22   2009023379

Editorial Credits
Jennifer Besel, editor; Veronica Bianchini, designer; Marcie Spence,
    media researcher; Eric Manske, production specialist;
    Sarah Schuette, photo stylist; Marcy Morin, scheduler

Photo Credits
All photos by Capstone Studio/Karon Dubke

The Capstone Press Photo Studio thanks Dance Express in
Mankato, Minnesota, for their help with photo shoots for this book.

Note to Parents and Teachers

The Dance, Dance, Dance series supports national physical education standards and the
national standards for learning and teaching dance in the arts. This book describes and
illustrates tap dancing. The images support early readers in understanding the text. The
repetition of words and phrases helps early readers learn new words. This book also introduces
early readers to subject-specific vocabulary words, which are defined in the Glossary section.
Early readers may need assistance to read some words and to use the Table of Contents,
Glossary, Read More, Internet Sites, and Index sections of the book.

Table of Contents

All about Tap

Make some noise

with your feet!

Move to the music

with tap dance.

Dancers use tap shoes

to stomp out beats

like a drummer.

is one thing... Dancing with the

7

Equipment

Tap shoes have metal pieces
on the toes and heels.
These pieces are called taps.

Tap shoes make loud sounds
against wood.
Dancers practice in studios
with wood floors.

DANCING with the feet is one thing... DANCING with th

Dancers wear costumes

during recitals.

All costumes let dancers

move easily.

Sweet Steps

Jump up and down

on one foot.

This move is called a hop.

one thing... DANCING w̶ Heart is Another

Strike your toes forward

on the floor.

This move is called a brush.

feet is one thing... DANCING with the Heart

Do the brush move

with one foot.

Then slide that foot back.

This step is called a shuffle.

Ready to Dance

Hop and shuffle

to the beat.

Now you're tap dancing!

Glossary

beat — the rhythm of a piece of music

costume — clothes dancers wear during a recital

heel — the back part of your foot or shoe

practice — doing an action over and over to get better at a skill

recital — a show where people dance for others

strike — to hit with force

studio — a room or building where a dancer practices

Read More

Clay, Kathryn. *Jazz Dancing.* Dance, Dance, Dance. Mankato, Minn.: Capstone Press, 2010.

Dillman, Lisa. *Tap Dancing.* Get Going! Hobbies. Chicago: Heinemann, 2006.

Murphy, Liz. *A Dictionary of Dance.* Maplewood, N.J.: Blue Apple Books, 2007.

Internet Sites

FactHound offers a safe, fun way to find Internet sites related to this book. All of the sites on FactHound have been researched by our staff.

Here's all you do:

Visit *www.facthound.com*

FactHound will fetch the best sites for you!

Index

Word Count: 118
Grade: 1
Early-Intervention Level: 12